Defeating The Literacy Act Monster

Defeating The Literacy Act Monster

Hello, I'm Khloe! I am in the 2nd grade, and I love to read. I also love playing with my iPad, jumping on our trampoline, and playing with dolls alongside my little sister. My mom and dad read bedtime stories daily when I was younger. Now, I can lead bedtime stories and read books to my little sister. I hope this book inspires you to enjoy reading like my family and I do. I want to thank my teachers for helping make it easier to read by teaching me letter sounds and how to spell new words.

If you get stuck while reading, take a deep breath, say something positive to yourself, and ask for help.
- Khloe Barham

"I am brave, and I will keep trying!"

"I'm getting better every time I read!"

"It's okay to need help—that's how I grow!"

"I can do hard things—I never give up!"

"I'll take my time and figure it out!"

'It's okay to make mistakes, I'm learning!"

Once upon a time, a brave and adventurous girl named Khloe lived in a city called McCalla, Alabama. Khloe loved many things: playing outside with her friends, exploring new games on her iPad, and reading exciting books.

One sunny afternoon, as Khloe and her friends gathered in the neighborhood, they heard a loud rumble. "What's that noise?" one of Khloe's friends asked, peering around nervously.

"It sounds like the Literacy Act Monster!" another friend shouted, eyes wide with fear. Khloe heard her teachers and principal talk about the Literacy Act Monster in a meeting at school. The Literacy Act Monster was a fearsome creature that roamed the land, gobbling up all the books, making it harder for kids to pass their reading assessments.
Literacy Act Monster

But Khloe wasn't afraid. "We can defeat the
Literacy Act Monster!" she declared, standing tall
and confident. "And do you know how? By reading!"
Her friends looked puzzled. "Reading?" they echoed.
CLASS

"Yes, reading!" Khloe said with a smile. "Reading is the most powerful tool we have. It helps us learn new words understand stories, and unlock whole worlds of imagination. If we read a new fun book every day, we'll become super readers, strong enough to outsmart any monster!" The more books we read, the harder it is for the Literacy Act Monster to take them all.

With Khloe leading the way, the group set off on a quest to conquer the Literacy Act Monster. They visited the town library, where they discovered shelves upon shelves of magical books waiting to be explored. Each day, they picked out a new adventure from the abundance of options in the kids section.

As they read together, Khloe and her friends felt their reading skills growing stronger and stronger. They learned new words, practiced comprehension, and discovered the joy of getting lost in a good book. And with each page they turned, the Literacy Act Monster seemed to shrink smaller and smaller until it disappeared entirely.

On the day of the reading assessment, Khloe and her friends felt confident and prepared. They enthusiastically tackled the reading test, using their super-reading powers to breeze through the questions. And when the results came in, they cheered with delight: they had all passed with flying colors!

Khloe and her friends knew reading was their greatest superpower from that day on. They continued to explore new books, sharing their favorites with each other and inspiring others to join their reading adventures.

And as for the Literacy Act Monster? It was never seen again, and Khloe and her friends had proven that anything is possible with the power of reading.

So remember, dear friends, if your parents or teachers talk to you about the Literacy Act Monster, know that you, too, can defeat it by reading more. If you get stuck while reading, take a deep breath, say something positive to yourself, and ask for help. With each page you turn, you're one step closer to victory!

Scan the QR code below to learn more about the Alabama Literacy Act.

Reading 15 minutes a day will keep the Literacy Act Monster away.

www.ingramcontent.com/pod-product-compliance
Lightning Source LLC
Chambersburg PA
CBRC090749110726
48005CB00008B/1023